The Forest of Dean

'… A superb introduction to
the wonderful Forest of Dean and
everything that makes it special'*

* From the Foreword by Jan Royall

First published 2011 by Tanners Yard Press

Tanners Yard Press Church Road Longhope GL17 0LA
www.tannersyardpress.co.uk

British Library Cataloguing in Publication Data
A catalogue record for this book is available from the British Library

ISBN   978 0 9564 3582 8

Designed by Paul Manning
Printed and bound in Poland
Polskabook UK Ltd

PHOTO CREDITS

All photos by Chris Morris, except:

10, Woody Morris; 96, Jemma Scott; 97, Daisy Adam; 98 l, Bronte Williams; 98 r, Gemma Frankland; 99,
Shantelle Minchin; 100, Mary Watkins; 101, Amy Wilce; 107, Woody Morris; 126 (Big Ben), Diane Gorvin.

THE FOREST
OF
DEAN

Photographs by
CHRIS MORRIS

Foreword by Jan Royall

Preface

I moved to Gloucestershire in 1999, having spent most of my life working as a commercial photographer in London. With more time on my hands, and the Forest of Dean on my doorstep, I was able to ally my new skills in digital technology to my long-standing interest in industrial history. The result was a collection of photographs of Dean's old iron and coal sites, which were slowly fading away in the woods. In 2001, this body of work went on exhibition in Gloucester Guildhall, and in 2002, it became my first book, *Work in the Woods*.

By the next year, the Forest Bookshop in Coleford was asking me why I didn't consider a book of photography addressing a wider set of subjects. 'Not everyone thinks the only important issue in Dean is its industrial past.' I had to agree, and in 2003, *A Portrait of Dean* was published. Both these early books are now unavailable.

This book continues with new photography on the same themes. It also includes images from projects I have worked on over the past decade for the Forestry Commission and for Lakers School, and work from various exhibitions. There is less of the Forest itself, as *Dean's Big Oaks*, published in 2007, is still available.

The subject matter is intended to suggest the ongoing traditions and culture of the Forest. There are countless painters, sculptors, blacksmiths, 'commoners' and miners working in the woods: those included are my personal choice and represent the wide range of artists and artisans at work in the Dean. A fuller list is available at *www.bigartweb.net*.

The whole publishing project which began a decade ago depended on the new possibilities of digital photography. The two early books contain a slightly wilful showing-off of Photoshop effects – indeed, *A Portrait of Dean* is prefaced with the warning of 'personal photographs, sometimes stylised and idiosyncratic'. Ten years on, my extensive use of digital technique is seldom in evidence in the final image.

I am neither a writer nor an historian: this book is a portfolio of photographs, and, as in that previous preface, my claim is simply to reflect and celebrate a personal selection of the diverse features that make the Forest special.

Chris Morris
April 2011

Contents

Right: Pupils of Bream Primary school water the 'Nelson Oak', planted in 2005 to mark the bicentenary of the Battle of Trafalgar.
This sapling replaced the 'Hard-Up Tree', where unemployed miners waited in the hope of a day job.

FOREWORD

Thank you, Chris, for producing another portfolio of beautiful photographs of the Forest of Dean. This book reminds us that this land between two rivers is a very special place, with its glorious ancient forest, abundant orchards, important industrial heritage, vibrant traditions, customary privileges and a strong community with a wealth of talents.

The photographs are a celebration of landscape and life in the Forest: they give us a taste of our history and they introduce us to artists and artisans whose work is inspired by the beauty of our surroundings. They bring to our attention the many traditions that still thrive, and the people who keep them alive, from Freeminers and coracle-makers to the 'old tradition commoners' who still graze their sheep on the edges of the Forest. They enable us to get to know people and places too seldom seen.

Chris has done a brilliant job, not just in taking the photographs and putting together the portfolio, but in allowing us to accompany him on a journey from past to present – a journey in which, along the way, he has nurtured the talents of women and men, giving them new skills and confidence to strive for their aspirations.

The photographs are a visual link with the history and heritage upon which our unique community is built. They also demonstrate the diversity of our community in the twenty-first century, and the resilience of our people – we only have to look at Rich Daniels who led the HOOF ('Hands Off Our Forest') campaign.

For me – as for many Foresters – some of the photographs are of personal significance, whilst others open my eyes to new people and places, but they all provide an interesting new perspective. For people who are new to the area or passing through, this book is a superb introduction to the wonderful Forest of Dean and everything that makes it special.

Jan Royall*
A 'Daughter of Dean'

* Baroness Royall of Blaisdon is current Leader of
the Opposition in the House of Lords.

Between Two Rivers

As in my earlier book, *A Portrait of Dean*, the first part of this book portrays a journey round the perimeter of the Forest. There are several possible definitions of the Forest boundaries: from the twelfth century, it was 'the hundred of St Briavels', while in 1833, the 'statutory forest' was defined by marker stones. Today, the Forest of Dean is both a parliamentary constituency and a local government administrative area.

For the purposes of this book, I take none of those definitions too strictly, and treat the Dean as the area between the rivers Severn and Wye. For a northern edge to this triangle, I have followed a section of the A40, originally Thomas Telford's road to Milford Haven, before cutting across the hills to the Wye. Only a couple of locations fall outside this definition of the Dean.

Left: Glynn Bullock, the Forestry Commission's community officer, with a restored 'Statutory Forest' boundary stone.

Facing page: Canoeing at Symond's Yat on the River Wye.

Above: At Over, the last remnants of
the Severn Bore push upstream under
Thomas Telford's bridge, historically the
lowest crossing-point of the river.

To the west, after five miles of flat
farmland (*facing page*), Telford's toll
house at Huntley (*left*) marks a choice
of routes to Monmouth.

From Huntley, the A40 avoids the Forest
by crossing a shoulder of the outlying May
Hill (*left*, and see pages 46-48), heading
for Ross-on-Wye. The alternative route
takes on the Forest hills. Our boundary
follows the Herefordshire line, to reach the
Wye north of Lydbrook.

Facing page: In his Lydbrook garden,
Tim Oakes, musician, storyteller and witch,
repairs a traditional coracle.

Left: Two centuries ago, the beauty of the Wye Valley inspired the poet Wordsworth and helped give birth to the modern notion of tourism. This view of the Wye is taken from Symonds Yat Rock, looking towards Wales.

Above: Painted cut-outs help the many 'twitchers' who flock to this viewpoint to identify the birds of prey nesting in the adjacent crags.

Above: The east and west banks of the
Wye at Symonds Yat are linked by a
rope-operated hand ferry.

Further downriver, the Kymin, opposite Monmouth, (*above*) was originally built as a gentlemen's dining club. When Nelson visited in 1802, he was mixing pleasure with business: his travelling companions were Lord and Lady Hamilton, and his business was selecting Forest oaks for the Navy.

Far right: Just before Chepstow, Tintern Abbey provides the valley's focal point.

Right: Detail of Bigsweir bridge.

At Chepstow (*left*), a wide bend sweeps the river below the castle ruins.

Below: By the old bridge, Simon Field still works in the woodyard set up by his father.

Facing page: At Beachley, the southernmost point of the Dean, the old ferry ramp still stands, made redundant by the first Severn Bridge, spanning both rivers, which towers overhead.

The Forest's original harbour was at Bullo Pill, a tiny creek near Newnham. The thick seam of coal dust deposited at the original ground level, revealed by recent ground clearance (*left*), marks the spot where barges were once filled with coal from chutes on the quayside.

Below: At Purton on the south bank of the Severn, old barges were sunk to reinforce the banks of the Sharpness Canal.

Facing page: Bullo was overtaken by much more extensive wharves at Lydney. Beside the surviving pier, tidal locks, now restored, lead from the river.

Above: At Awre (see page 121**)**, fisherman fix their rows of 'putchers' for trapping salmon.

Right: Downstream at Newnham, water skiers and surfers clamber on to their boards, hoping to ride the tidal phenomenon of the Severn Bore all the way to Over Bridge.

Facing page: The Severn's huge horseshoe meander at Newnham is seen from the viewpoint of Blaize Bailey.

LANDSCAPE AND LEGACY

This section falls into three main parts. The first explores Dean's changing landscape, from prehistoric times, through the Roman occupation, to the days of the tramway, railways and nineteenth-century water management. Two further sections are gleaned from exhibitions: May Hill is a favourite local landmark for me, and has been the subject of several shows in the Post Office Gallery in Longhope, where I live. The photographs of Shakemantle, a worked-out quarry, date from 2008, and have been exhibited at Taurus Crafts at Lydney and at the Nature in Art gallery and museum at Twigworth.

Left: The rebuilt shaft of New Fancy mine; the spoil tip a hundred metres to the south provides a fine Forest viewpoint.

Right: Miners' memorial in Cinderford town centre; sculpture by Antony Dufort.

Above: Jon Hoyle of Gloucester Archaeology assesses a newly discovered Bronze Age circle near Woolaston *(top right)*, which includes these three regularly spaced small standing stones.

Right: Strata in Hobbs Quarry show limestone running over a baulk of coral that once thrived in a warm sea.

Facing page: The ramparts and ditches of the Iron Age fort at Welshbury Hill are visually softened by the timber cover.

Above: The Dean Road at Blackpool Bridge is believed to form part of a Roman route from Lydney to Weston-under-Penyard. It has since been treated to a very inferior re-surfacing.

Facing page: The Roman temple at Lydney Park included a large courtyard hostel for visiting pilgrims and an elaborate bath suite. The outline of the courtyard and the supporting tile stacks of the hypocaust (*right*) are still intact today.

Above: At Knockley a railway crosses an earlier tramway route, and the tunnel is one of few that remain acccessible.

Right: The packhorse bridge near to Dean Heritage Centre in Soudley indicates the line of the original route up the valley.

Above: These stones originally bore the rails of a
tramway leading up Bixslade to the stone quarries.

In its industrial heyday, the Forest was riddled with mine and quarry tramways which were eventually replaced by connected rail routes. The Dean Forest Railway (*right*) runs on a restored route from Lydney to Parkend. Other routes have been turned into cycleways (*top right*).

Above: The only funicular railway in the Forest is in this Longhope garden, where it is used to carry materials from the track end to the higher cottage level.

Above: The great railway engineer Isambard Kingdom Brunel took his South Wales main line most picturesquely along the Severn from Gloucester to Chepstow (see page 34).

As well as the South Wales main line, Brunel was responsible for turning the Forest tracks acquired by the Great Western into 'broad gauge'. Bridges still remain on the route to Ross, but the line is largely shadowed pasture (*left*).

The huge piece of black tubing (*above*) was until recently on view in a Chepstow engineering yard, and is a section of the original bridge over the Wye. The decorative column capital in Chepstow station (*top*) is typical of Brunel's design for the GWR.

Above: Remnants of Brunel's distinctive 'top-hat'
section rail can be seen on many old Forest lines,
used as fence posts.

In mining terrain, water was both an asset and a dangerous nuisance. Many streams and ditches were canalised with stone-built walls and floors to carry water to ponds – initially as headers for the leats supplying water wheels, and later as a resource for the steam engines. At the same time, conserving the water meant there was less likelihood of it seeping into the mine workings.

The photos show a flooded tramway at Knockley (*top left*), Soudley Brook (*top right*), Ropehouse Ditch in Sallowvallets (*right*), a dry section of Blackpool Brook (*facing page*), the water wheel at the Dean Heritage Centre, originally a mill (*bottom left*), and a sluice at Cannop Colliery (*left*).

A variety of flowers thrive in Dean's ancient woodlands. Pictured here are orchids near Wigpool (*right*), wood anenomes and wild daffodils in Oxenhall Wood (*above*), and bluebells at Bradley Hill (*facing page*).

Plum orchards once completely lined the Longhope Valley from Blaisdon to May Hill, and the many remnants light up with spring blossom.

These views are of orchards at Little London, with sheep (*below*), lit by strong evening sun (*left*), and finally at dusk, with crows (*facing page*).

Previous page: Shakemantle Quarry has been disused since the early 1970s.

The photos on this page are from a set in which I used digital techniques to reinforce the sense of abandonment and isolation of this huge old quarry.

May Hill, outstanding to the north of Longhope, is higher than the Forest's highest point at Ruardean. Visible from miles away in all directions, it has a 360-degree vision from the summit, which is crowned with a grove of Corsican pines planted to celebrate Queen Victoria's golden jubilee.

Earthworks on the hill include ancient boundary banks (with thorn hedge remnant, *right*) and a ring ditch around the summit suggestive of an ancient camp.

Above: Ponies graze free-range on May Hill. The views in the snow (*left*) and with sheep (*facing page*) are taken from Chessgrove Lane, Longhope.

The Industrial Past

This chapter is largely drawn from my earlier book *Work in the Woods* and shows the remaining structures of the iron mining and working that was Dean's most important industry, and some of the remains of the subsequent deep-pit coal mining. New photographs celebrate the most significant site, Darkhill ironworks, and its associated experimental works, known as the Titanic steelworks.

Until the latter part of the seventeenth century, the Dean was Britain's most important site for iron foundries, but the industry was curtailed by royal decree in order to keep the oaks for shipbuilding, rather than using the timber for charcoal. Abraham Darby's discovery that coke was a better iron-making fuel gave Coalbrookdale pre-eminence. However, it triggered the production of coal (for conversion to coke) in Dean, where furnaces again had an important role to play. At Darkhill, David Mushet and his son, Robert Forester Mushet, experimented with steel production. Although Henry Bessemer is widely credited with the invention of steel-making, his method would have failed without the modification provided by Robert Mushet.

Above: The miners' memorial at Bixslade, by sculptor Matt Baker, is sited on the shaft of Union Mine, where four men died in underground floods in 1902. *Facing page*: The bridge and south portal of the tunnel at Mirystock. The north portal has also been cleared, but the tunnel cannot be used as part of the cycle route for 'health and safety' reasons.

Puzzle Wood (*above*) is one of several areas in the Forest where small-scale cliffs, ravines, arches and caves are thought to be the ancient remains of iron ore scavenging. Recent claims suggest that these ground shapes may be due to water erosion, and any iron ore-gathering incidental.

What is certain is that Clearwell Caves have been dug for iron ore since pre-Roman times. The Drummer Boy Stone (*right*) is said to show traces of iron working. It is possible that the hollow on its surface is from use as a grinding stone, and that the stone was co-incidentally used in a furnace.

Facing page: Rather like a Mediterranean peasant harvesting olives by shaking the tree, in Clearwell Caves, Ray Wright gathers ochre, valuable as a pigment, by scraping it from the ceiling to collect on polythene sheeting.

Gunns Mill, near Flaxley, (*left*), was a seventeenth-century charcoal-fired iron furnace. Ten years ago, it was thought that the timber superstructure was added when the furnace was turned into a paper mill. Recent carbon dating has shown that the timbers are of the same date as that cast on the furnace lintel.

For the last ten years, the building has been shrouded in a polythene tent while the archaeologists ponder a new move – or maybe wait for funds.

Facing page: Whitecliff, close to Coleford, is important as an early coke-fired iron furnace, associated with David Mushet (see pages 56–9).

Previous page: Darkhill ironworks was a key site in the development of the iron and steel industries.

On first arriving in the Dean, the Scottish ironmaster David Mushet worked the Whitecliff furnace (see page 55). Later, he established a coke-fired furnace at Darkhill, where he and his son Robert Forester Mushet pioneered the development of steel-making.

After his father's death, Robert set up a new site just to the north at Gorsty Knoll which he named Titanic. Here, his experimental work was to lead him to an involvement with Henry Bessemer, the man credited with the invention of steel. Mushet's work made a vital contrbution to Bessemer's process, but in business terms he was outflanked and cheated: it seems odd that, to this day in Britain, he remains almost unknown, whereas schoolchildren in the USA learn the science under the title, the 'Bessemer-Mushet Process'.

Right: It was Robert Mushet's Titanic steelworks that in 1857 produced the world's first steel railway track. Appropriately, The Mushets' memorial is a simple section of steel rail.

By 2001, Darkhill was already recognised as an important site. At that time, much of the land to the north of it was a tangle of creeper-clad forest, but through the undergrowth, I was able to notice the overgrown archway and comment, 'This does not look like a remnant of a cottage outbuilding – I believe it is Titanic'. Today, the whole area has been cleared by the Forestry Commission, and the two huge gable ends have appeared as if by magic (*above*), where before nothing was visible amongst the trees. The archway (*facing page*, photographed in 2001) has also been restored (*left*).

Above: The ruin of an old engine house marks Fairplay Shaft, the entrance to an iron mine at the top of Plump Hill. Further along the ridge at Wigpool, Ken Durham (*left*) lives in what was once the office of the mine where his father worked. Outside, on proud display, is the 'kibble', or large bucket, used to transport men and materials up and down the shaft.

Facing page: The iconic Findall chimney stands high on Staple Edge, a ridge over the upper Soudley valley. The updraft from a fire in its ground-level hearth was able to ventilate the Perseverance iron mine deep below.

Top left: Opposite the Dilke hospital in Cinderford, a timber yard occupies the site of the former Lightmoor deep colliery. Remaining buildings include the engine house (*left*). The beam engine (*above*), on display at Dean Heritage Centre, worked on this site.

Facing page: Zion Baptist Chapel, Soudley, built as solid and square as an engine house, is also in the care of Dean Heritage Centre.

Above: Paid for partly by miners' subscriptions, Princess Royal bath house was the finest of four built in the Forest in 1944. Its importance in social history and as an example of modernist architectural style was completely ignored when it was scheduled for demolition in 2002. A subsequent campaign in 2003 succeeded in saving it from the bulldozers, but after years of wrangling and side-stepped promises, it was finally knocked down in 2010. The ornate tile (*facing page*) is not from the bath house itself, but from the offices across the road, which are still standing.

Left: At Eastern United colliery, Ruspidge, a heap of brick rubble is all that remains of one of the other three bath houses; the two remaining, at Cannop and Northern United, are seriously altered examples.

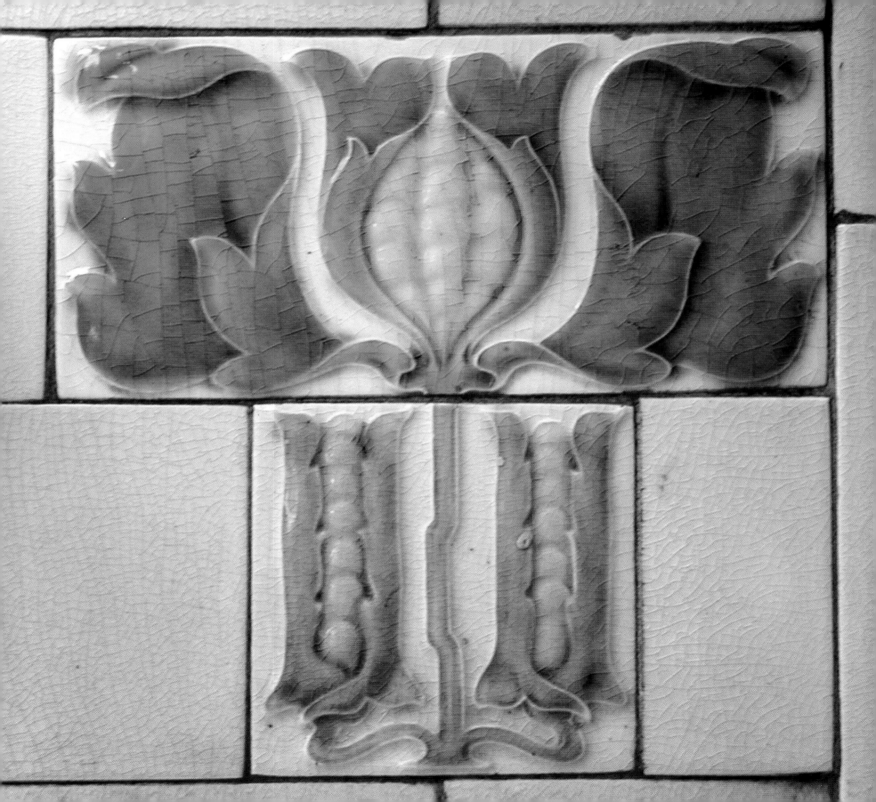

Above: A weighbridge stands amongst the desolate jumble of buildings at Northern United, the last big pit to close, on Christmas Eve, 1965.

Facing page: The small brick buildings, tucked away in the woods 100 metres west of Cannop's old colliery complex, look a little like outside loos, but were in fact magazines for storing gunpowder.

Perhaps the best memorials to Dean's deep-mining past are the spoilheaps which rise like giant tree-covered molehills out of the woods. They are a humbling sight, a large-scale visual reminder of the sweat and toil underground that created them.

These 2001 photographs show the tips at Cannop (*left and facing page, bottom left*) and at Northern United (*below left*) and the Forest's last remaining winding wheel frame at Parkend Royal, now lost (*facing page, bottom right*).

ART AND ARTISANS

The Forest of Dean has always attracted artists to live and work in its idyllic woodlands, as well as providing inspiration for local talent. The first part of this chapter shows some of the works on the Sculpture Trail which begins at the Forestry Commission's centre, Beechenhurst Lodge. For several years, I have run spring and summer courses in digital photography here, and some of the participants feature in the photographs reproduced here.

In 2002, the Forestry Commission arranged, as an experiment, to offer oak 'thinnings' (which would otherwise have been turned into wood pulp) free of charge to artists and woodworkers. The condition was that a piece had to be available for a touring exhibition, and that I would be able to photograph both the woodworkers themselves and their work. Of the thirty-odd photos that travelled with the exhibition, very few have so far been published, and a selection appears here, mostly for the first time, supplemented with some ten-year updates.

To balance the inclusion of the woodworkers, in spring of this year I took the opportunity to photograph some of Dean's artists working in various other disciplines.

Above: The huge wooden chair, 'Place' by Magdalena Jetelová (see page 77), is the first sculpture on the trail leading from Beechenhurst Lodge.

Facing page: Taurus Crafts at Lydney has a range of activities and includes a sculpture yard (see pages 86 and 90).

Above: Sited in a damp hollow and sometimes lapped by water, the pieces which make up 'Fire and Water Boats' by David Nash appear to be hewn out of single tree trunks.

Facing page: 'Cathedral' by Kevin Atherton is a huge stained-glass window hanging in a broad avenue of pines. The side supports are reminiscent of pit head frame structures.

'Echo'. by Annie Cattrell (on the scaffolding, *right*) is a same-size casting of the tiny scale quarry seen in the background. These photographs are from a commission by the Sculpture Trust to show the stages of constuction, using latex rubber and fibreglass, undertaken by art workers Lisa Scantlebury and Mark Plenderleith (*far right and below*). The final casting was in a metallic resin.

Established in 1986, the Forest of Dean Sculpture Trail was one of the first of its kind to open in the UK.

One of the first pieces on view, rearing through the wooded skyline, is 'Place' by Magdalena Jetelová (*facing page*). On this occasion, the giant chair, with its view across Cannop valley, is framed by the figures of camera-wielding students on my digital photography course.

Above: 'Searcher', a wire deer by Sophie Ryder, has ben given a little Photoshop tweak to suggest motion.

Left: An entire oak tree was felled and turned to a cube to create 'Raw', by Neville Gabie. The piece sits in the clearing, the space once occupied by the tree, whose scale can be judged by the adjacent stump left in the ground.

'Dead Wood – Bois Mort' by Carole Drake (*facing page*) has a very low-key presence, flat amongst the debris of the forest floor, but a lot of 'second glance' detail. 'Melissa's Swing' by Peter Appleton (*above*) provides light relief for the juniors on the trail.

'Cathedral', 'Fire and Water Boats', 'Place' and 'Raw' were all photographed as a commission for the Sculpture Trust, for reproduction as postcards.

In 2002, the Forestry Commission, wondering whether there was a better use for oak 'thinnings' than mere woodpulp, gave away a quantity of green oak to artists and woodworkers. The selection of photographs here come from a collection of more than 30 which accompanied the resulting work on a travelling exhibition.

Left: Although his partner Mervyn Bic (pictured right) has now retired, Gilbert Crawford still makes fine furniture at Bilbec Design workshop, Staunton and Corse.

David Gooding (*below*), then and now primarily a sculptor in metal, had no idea what to make: I recently caught up with him at Brains Greeen and watched him finishing off an intricate bronze (*right*).

Above: The mirror Andrew Darke made in 2002 might look very plain, but there is a twist in the tale: the intention was that the green oak frame would in time warp, causing the stainless steel mirror surface to distort.

On a recent re-visit, I was able to look at Andrew's ongoing experimental project, where 5-7 metre tall wands anchored in a pond twist and turn in the slightest breeze (*right*). The work is perhaps best appreciated by looking at video clips on his website.

Conceptual artist Helen Schell (*left*), despite not being a woodworker, made herself a throne, and looks suitably regal with it. She now works in Sunderland.

Top right: Phil Bews has a nationwide reputation as a woodcarver, but is best known in the Forest for his 'fire sculptures' (see page 126).

Above: If conceptual artists can make furniture, why shouldn't furniture designers make sculpture? Jonathan Harrison, photographed in 2001 (*facing page, bottom right*), is a furniture designer from Newent. He has recently been working on a memorial bench for ex-council chairman, the late George Read, sited above Mitcheldean on Plump Hill.

Right: Painter Doug Eaton, whose Forest family stretches back many generations, works in a room of his Mile End house. His paintings, based on landscape themes, have been traditional, but he has recently adopted a more fundamental approach to shape and colour, best described as semi-abstract.

Above: Mary Edwards works in the kitchen of her isolated farmhouse near Bigsweir. Her tiny impressionistic paintings mostly refer back to her late husband and to memories of working with animals on the farm.

Above: Carrie Horwood was the first female apprentice to complete her training at Gloucester Cathedral stonemasons' yard. She is now successfully based at Taurus Crafts in Lydney.

Clare Robertson (*facing page*) works from the blacksmith's shop at Clearwell Caves, making decorative art pieces – and definitely not horseshoes.

Above: Ron Boyd lives on Ruardean Hill. He has been painting rural scenes for decades and his work is often seen in Forest venues. His large canvases with their intricate detail can take him months to complete.

Sally Stafford begins her paintings quite conventionally, applying broad brushstrokes to a canvas on an easel. She then puts the canvas on the floor, and, apparently in a trance-like state, moves rapidly around it, spattering acrylic colour from bottles. After softening the effect with wash, she adds more detail, until, as if by magic, a wonderful field of wild flowers is created, which is then left to dry under heaters. Sally works at Harts Barn craft centre and sells her paintings through a gallery in Monmouth.

Above: Mike Penny is chairman and a founder member of Clay Hill Potters, a group of enthusiasts who share well-equipped workshops in converted farm buildings on a hill overlooking the river at Newnham.

Below: At Taurus Crafts, Martin Stephens is in charge of the pottery, where children's sessions are available.

Above: Steve Hyslop, stained glass artist and woodcut printmaker, lives and works on a boat on the Severn at Bullo Pill. The work he is holding is a woodcut of the American folk singer Woody Guthrie.

Mollie Meager has a long track record for her stained glass work. Here, she displays a piece outside her Pillowell workshop and kiln, newly built using straw bale technology.

DAUGHTERS OF DEAN

In 2008, following a term working with pupils at Bream Primary, I was offered a new project at Lakers School. The idea of 'Daughters of Dean', which I had been nursing for a couple of years, was to celebrate the achievements of women who had grown up in the Forest.

The rationale was that Dean's history tends to be dominated by 'macho male' activities. The proposal was to take a series of photos that would address the misconception that a woman's role is just to mind the house or work behind the counter. Headteacher Alison Elliott saw the project as an opportunity to create aspirational awareness, and I became a tutor to a dozen Year 10 girls every Friday afternoon. Between us, we chose a dozen subjects to photograph in appropriate locations. The project ended with an exhibition at Taurus Crafts in Lydney.

Right: Children at Bream Primary celebrate the oak trees in their own school grounds.

Facing page: Year 9 girls at Lakers have fun in the adjacent forest, learning camera skills.

94

Facing page: The late Lady Edna Healey grew up in Coleford and attended Bell's Grammar School, where she was the first to win a scholarship to Oxford. Edna kindly wrote a foreword to *A Portrait of Dean* and I returned the favour by taking this photograph of her in the bluebells at Bradley Hill for her autobiography, *Part Of The Pattern*, published in 2006.

Andrea McLean (*above*) also grew up in Coleford and has achieved great acclaim as an artist. I met her when she was artist in residence at Gloucester Cathedral, but this photograph was taken during a year which she spent living and working in a farmhouse in the Black Mountains.

These two photographs became the inspiration for the 'Daughters of Dean' project, as described on the previous page. The photographs on the following pages are all by Year 10 girls at Lakers School.

Above: Jemima Phillips, harpist,
by Daisy Adams.

Left: Kate Biggs, industrial archaeologist,
by Jemma Scott.

Above: Morgan Williams,
gymnast, by Bronte Williams.

Right: Georgia Stevens, England rugby player,
by Gemma Frankland.

Facing page: Maggie Clutterbuck, poet
and performer, by Shantelle Minchin.

Above: Pauline Nash, interior designer, by Mary Watkins.

Right: Mary Rose Young, potter, by Amy Wilce.

CONTINUUM

This final chapter focuses on many more of the ongoing local traditions that make the communities of Dean special. As in my earlier book, *A Portrait of Dean*, images of fathers and sons underline the sense of continuity. Applicants wishing to qualify for the Forest's unique title of 'Freeminer' must have been born within the 'Hundred of St Briavels' (a Forest definition dating back to the thirteenth century), and must have worked underground in the Hundred for at least a year and a day. The requirement to be male has been overturned, albeit with some dispute, and the Forest now has its first female Freeminer, Elaine Morman. Mining in the Dean is controlled by the 'deputy gaveller'. The post is vacant at the time of writing, and day-to-day issues are taken care of by the assistant, James Britten (see page 108).

Since the eleventh century, the Dean has been subject, not to common law like the rest of Britain, but to 'forest law'. Local issues and disputes are settled in the Verderers' Court, which still meets four times a year in the courtroom of the Speech House Hotel.

Above: Diana Smart making cheese at Birdwood.

Facing page: Fallen apples in an orchard, The Lea.

In the year 2000, my first contact with freeminers was with Gerald Haynes (*above*). After decades of single-handedly working a mine known as Hayners Bailey (*top right*), Gerald retired in 2001.

Mervyn Bradley (*right*) had been on the cusp of getting coal from Lydbrook Deep, but abandoned it that same year, going on to work at Gerald's old mine, renamed Monument (as Matt Baker's memorial, pictured on page 50, was close by).

Above: At Hamblins Yorkley, John Hine's group, long since disbanded, mixed optimism with a social night out: a little light labour was followed by a brew-up, before the group retired to the Rising Sun at Mosley Green.

Robin Morgan (*left*) has for a whole decade presided over his mine museum at Hopewell; stoic and steadfast, the eternal optimist, Robin is always about to bring coal up to market.

Keeping track of the freeminers is hard: their comings and goings seem a little like a game of musical chairs, with miners constantly moving from site to site, and mines opening and closing. In 2001, Ray Ashley (*above*) shut down his own drift mine, Quidchurch, on Staple Edge (*below*), and went with Mervyn Bradley to Monument. Mervyn's son Mark joined in, then later, Ray left the team.

By 2007, Mervyn and Mark (*left*) had themselves left Monument; Ray had moved back and was joined by Rich Daniels and Neil Jones (*facing page*). Mervyn had moved up the track behind the mine and was, and still is, running a quarry there (see page 110).

Above: In 2011, further up the valley, Ray Ashley's son runs Cannop Drift and is said to be opening up another productive mine higher up the slad. Above, half hidden behind the bushes, is the corrugated shed of Hamblins Yorkley, where John Hine's group met to dig and brew up ten years earlier (see page 105).

Above: Another part-time team, twins Richard and Stephen Harding, are also sure they are on to a good seam of coal, opening up into old workings above Heywood School in Cinderford.

Top left: Eric Morris, president of the Freeminers Association, proudly shows off his personal trophy, the works steam whistle from the Northern United colliery in Cinderford (see page 110).

Facing page, bottom: Today, Robin Morgan is still about to get coal from Hopewell. Phoenix (*above*), another part of his network of entrances, is run on a part-time basis by assistant deputy gaveller James Britten.

Above: Mervyn Bradley clears topsoil in his quarry in Bixslade.

Right: Eric Morris, President of the Freeminers, has, like Mervyn Bradley, come up into the daylight to run Astonbridge Hill quarry. He is pictured here with his stepson (*right*) and grandson (*left*).

Facing page: These Bixslade quarrymen were photographed in 2001. The quarry continues to supply the stone factory (see next page), but only one of the original team still works there.

Above: This view of the massive corrugated-iron roof of the stone factory in the Cannop valley dates back to 2001. At that time, the cutting machinery inside the shed had been unchanged for a century (*facing page*). The system of shafts, belts and cogs was originally driven by steam, and the crane driver's cabin (*left*) had its own separate steam engine.

In its place now is a totally new factory, but a nod to tradition is its use of water power (*right*). Some of the plant's power is supplied by a turbine driven by the leat that originally served a huge water wheel at Parkend.

Left: Photographed in 2001, the congregation of Edge End chapel, now closed.

Above: Also at Edge End, the remains of New Found Out mine, near Lakers School.

Above: Don Burgess runs the 'Freeminers Brewery' in Cinderford. Originally a local concern, it now has national distribution.

Right: Apple-crushing millstone, Dean Heritage Centre.

Facing page: Father and son, Ray and Andy Tosh, cider makers, Blaize Bailey.

In the Forest, 'commoners' enjoy the right to graze animals on forest verges and other common land. Most are small landowners who 'turn out' their sheep, but bring them in for lambing or for other reasons. Farmers who follow the 'old tradition' rely totally on common ground for grazing their flock.

Mick Holder and Henry Mills (*facing page*) are secretary and chairman of the Forest Commoners Association, which celebrates its centenary in 2011.

Top right: Ben Hancocks 'badgering' sheep at Sallowvallets, 2002. Foresters use the term to describe a shepherd moving sheep from place to place.

Right: 'Old tradition commoners' Bev Turpin-West and her daughters Tilly and Poppy, with four of their sheep at The Pludds, 2011. *Top left*: Tilly helps Poppy treat a lamb with an injured foot.

Facing page: Father and son Chris and Chris Cadogan with a salmon at their 'putchers' (see page 22), near Awre on the Severn.

Left: Gordon Macdonald retired from the RAF to become self-sufficient on his one-acre plot at Ellwood. The vegetable beds in the front garden are reminiscent of the TV sitcom 'The Good Life'. As well as chickens, Gordon raises batches of three Old Spot pigs twice a year.

Below: Tilly Turpin-West with a lamb. All the ewes in her small flock are named; the lambs, soon destined for the dinner table, are not.

Facing page: In this photograph from 2002, Dave Bradley, Cinderford rugby club's under-13 team coach, harangues his squad, including his son Dane (second from right). Nine years later, Dockham Road's tiny yet iconic grandstand remains (despite Tesco), and Dane still plays rugby for Cinderford.

Canoeing (*above*) is a big sport on the Wye. The woods of the Dean are a favourite venue for orienteering (*left*); this 2002 shot shows Woody Morris collecting up race markers at Sallowvallets.

At the beginning of 2011, a government threat to sell off forests provoked widespread outrage in the Dean. A protest campaign, 'Hands Off Our Forest' (HOOF), culminated with large crowds braving the snow to attend a rally and march. The Forest of Dean brass band played (*facing page*), and stirring oratory was heard at Speech House. A Phil Bews fire sculpture of Big Ben was burned (*above*); Phil modestly points out that credit for the sculpture should not be his alone, as he depended on a dedicated 'build and burn' team.

A few weeks later, a triumphant second rally celebrated a 'U-turn' from Westminster. Baroness Royall ceremoniously removed a HOOF banner from the trees (*left*), and Rich Daniels, miner, activist and chairman of HOOF, gave a victory address in front of Speech House (*top left*).

Above: Brinchcombe from Staple Edge.

Index to 'Brown Sign' Sites

Index to Other Locations

Figures in brackets are **OS** grid references.

Index to Artists, Artisans and 'Daughters of Dean'

Acknowledgements

Particular thanks to my editor and designer Paul Manning; to Jan Royall for her very generous foreword, and to Ben Lennon of the Forestry Commission for help and advice.

My thanks also go to all those who agreed to appear in the book; to Diane Gorvin, Woody Morris and to the girls from Lakers for the use of their photos, and to the 'brown-sign' sites for their co-operation.